POEMS BY DANIEL HABERMAN

POEMS

By DANIEL HABERMAN

DRAWINGS BY
CORNELIA BRENDEL FOSS

NEW YORK
ART DIRECTION BOOK COMPANY
1977

Art Direction Book Company,
19 West 44 Street, New York City 10036

Library of Congress catalog card number: 76-56618
ISBN: 0-910158-24-X
Copyright © 1977 by Daniel Haberman

Printed in the United States of America

for Edward

CONTENTS

You are doubtless like myself; you have the same

terrifying & tedious depths.

Gustave Flaubert

THE FLUTED BIRD

Inside me:
A dog barks all night
On a country winter road.
A fluted bird
Comes to visit me
As friends are often want.
Then I'd walk
Back along the path
And trod the ways from which we came.

One may watch a geranium grow
And even sigh a reverie
Upon another reverie;
And then undrossed
Watch a flower
Explicate

A LETTER TO EDWARD DAHLBERG

No. I'd not want to be a poet:
Cross the abyss to carrion sea;
Sailing where hateful extremity flows—
No longer wombly hid near Lethe's shore.

This shore invites no newly suffered thought:
Activity provides the opiate—
How secure to dwell in forgetfulness
And exchange mere feeling for euphemism.

Now. From playing lands I'd spleen the shoreless sea
And flow where flouting ambivalents flowed,
On the distend waters of reverie—
No longer wombly hid near Lethe's shore.

Do we have such secrets to keep within;
Or would you agree we share them all?
In madcap times I have hidden
The strangest thoughts
Beside a public wall.

I fear the forest of my Fortressed heart;
Beyond the lurching days when love may end:
Where cavernous time bewilders me
And scolds the member that won't mend.

A PILGRIMED SOUL

There is a time of unsweet regress.

Who then believes in coincidence
With sophistication beyond our years?
Temptation rises to hate that womb;
    And stay the time when I appeared
    To love the world in innocence.
That bloated carnage scowls me mute;
And what innocence dared not demand
Cast round my scanned and pilgrimed soul.

THE PRISONER

I'm the prisoner of my poem—
For music heard I am denied:
I must pay—I must pay—
For my poem I will pay!

It is the agent of my rage
And—night-hounded—I am confined
To the smallest ward of all—
The pacing prison of my mind!

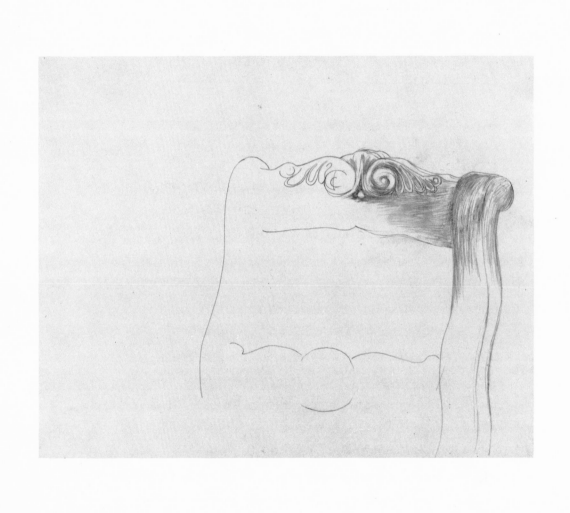

SONNET IN THE WAR METER

If I write a poem; is it not mine to keep?
Do I really have to share it? intruded on.
Unsharing; I'm an expert at living alone
And dueling with slow silence in the thorough day.
Euphony-loved and book-cared, though empty delight,
I'm not at all sure I'd want to be with me!
I have many thoughts I no longer share,
Since he secreted them to a distant time.
He carried off my secrets to a garish maze
(No less unkind—not knowing he'd impaired).
Exposed as Isaac: I stood upon a stage
And, laughter besieged, I began to live unshared.
Do we all share such secrets when we failing-care?
Do I live alone, and unsharing, share?

There's a rotting in me grows;
A bulbing canker of the soul.

At my peril I'd unearth it;
There's a rotting in me grows.

UNKIND REALITY

I numbed the world in fear of feeling.

And now I, too, am too much in the sun:
Gasping, I grasp the bottom of the earth;
Bloated, my bleeding hands are cleaving
                                    to the earth—
                    Now unkind reality
                    Observes the baleful fantasy:
Is death the only shield right for me?
Glistening, the garish sun makes mutants
                                    of my thoughts;
Burning, the accidental sun rages—
And there are no rocks to shield me, while cleaving
                                    to the earth.

The other day—near Loitering Hill—
Green by the grass—in pranced review—
I saw my past—and pondered why
It was to be my future too.

Yet flames hawk about the loitering log—
Then who sees not the poet's sight;
But amend their dreams in the coddling night...

SOLILOQUY

Falstaff looked in a glass
And saw (in his opinion),
Grace and beauty and integrity.
When I look in a glass,
Whom do I see?
Whose eyes peer back?
Are there two of us standing here
Separate from the other?
Is it Falstaff I find
Peering back?
Alone I would peer
And alone I would see:
For aloneness is the mirror
That summons careful agony
And witnesses the want.

16

Reflecting here in my opinion
(If I had an opinion),
I'd wash the glass snow-white;
And let him sleep away
On a crusted night.

Are ears
Still to be
    receptacles
(For tears)
 While lying on my back?

Now time drifts and worlds whine
By the weeds of inanition—
Which skive my soul paring down:
Rutting things shed themselves
Like a craning vine in keening soil.

SONNET UNRHYMED

An unruly thing when no place to go:
The quiet of my house is heard within.
Indicters surround in blowsy air
And clones disquiet the dull days...
Truth is: not for me are books to breathe;
I'll not be allowed to invent my time!
I'm but a madman: squatting naked
In the nearing night—wondering why...
Shivering in fear of banality,
My mimetic mind has garbaged away
How many poems that feed the gulls
Newly carrion thoughts of small despair...
Then I walk wanton in a gaping wood
And wear a mantle of laughing words.

Like a flouting spider
Percipient pain
Blends a beaded weave
With knowledge—
And snares
Emerging revelation

intimate

intimāte

intimidate

intimist

intimate

VISITING DAUBER & PINE BOOK SHOP INC.

More books! I
Must have more books—
And surround myself with
A wall erected to an
Irrefrenable part; neatly
Mortared with small despair.

WHEN I WALK AMONG THE FLOWERS

Now I would like to anchor here—
And go ashore among the flowers.

But pirate courage are pistols;
And then conversation shallows;
And pauses are but silences—
When I walk among the flowers.

AT THE CHILDREN'S BEACH

I went sailing once,
    Beyond the curling sea!
And when I came to my own shore—
    . . . It staggered me.

With studded fear I gazed about,
    Not knowing what to do;
And strode the beach incessantly—
    But seeking only me.

I rubbed my eyes with wonderment:
    To see a man appear.
He was the kind to lose one's self—
    Then I exhausted fear.

And daffodils—cupped with tears—
    Now are waiting near.

SINGING

One world with time on two continuum.
On one, hours drag and years fly from;
Yet time's place is lost when work is liked:
May I sing as the songbird—rare in flight?

Though the byplay is often juxtaposed,
Measured success assumes a role;
Yet sleeps away on a crusted night.
    O please,
May I sing as the songbird—rare in flight?

Now. What am I going to do with me?
I'd make peace with the King of Thebes
And tedious Telemachus: seeking might.
(Starting false with accidental sight)
I'd sing as the songbird in rare flight!

I MEETING ME

Where goslings gaze they tumble out:
The tactile words skulk inside;
As there I greet another one,
Who skulked to where the goslings gaze.

Absenting conflict
May be sweet as when we see
The first shooting sprout
Of spring

Timbered memories
Flood the fungible tide
As then undammed
The poet rides the river;
And is not

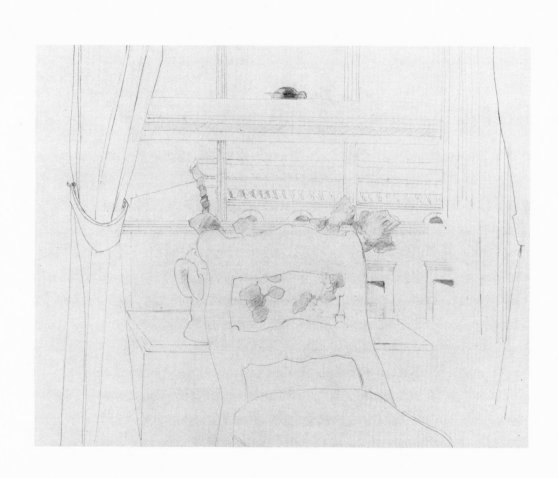

A CHANCE CONVERSATION WITH ROBERT FROST

To the fields of Tuscany I'd go,
Where no language barriers appear.
A hilltop higher to a mountain ridge,
Where I walk in the same field of yellow
And I drink from the same waterfall,
While my old friend the cuckoo reassures:
Farmers are farmers—daffodils yellow;
Apple blossoms still blossom whitest white.
I have never seen a more gentle place,
Though I think I've been here many times.
By an old old stream the map calls Nestor,
(Do you believe in coincidence?)
Horace provides the sweetest of pillows
And, one yellow buttercup in my hair,
I drift away in Tuscany. . .

"Poet: still alone?. . .What're you doing here?
 What's here in a field on a mountaintop;
 By old streams of Tuscany?"

"I remember a more gentle time,
 So languished by fleeted memory:
 I had picked nameless ones; and sprigs of
 Apple blossoms that blossom'd whitest white.
 Over there: beyond the stream called Nestor;
 Past the daisies—

                    '. . . a swinger of birches!
 Climbing limb by limb up a chestnut tree;
 Proud as only a young boy is smug
 When he's climbed the top of the tallest one. . .'
 A fertile time in a fertile field;
 When not yet smitten by puberty
 Or Romulus' fraternal night,
 He doesn't know he's climbed his highest height.
 Oh, you were right!. . . I think you were right."

"I don't know where it's likely to go better."

AWAKENING IN UMBRIA

Dawn. Hypnopompia's swirled
In defiant air . . .
What was I about?
Decisions made long ago:
Either way, what do I know?
But—I'll decide what to do
After I've done it.
We've all read little
And have much to say . . .
But do not despise me
For not knowing; nor
        for knowing . . .
I'm gorged with inconsistencies
And grope strange paths.

Why war with you and rage about?

The saddened time interferes
        with joy; and
Overbounds old-found woe...
Who is not but a madman
Squatting in his asylum house?
Cruelty is not brokered as
        your exclusive; nor
Has longing been foreclosed...
What are expectations but
Opening desire...
We do know—don't we?—
That he was right:
The heart is always inexperienced.

But you screamed at me yesterday...
        or so it seemed;
For what reason were you silent...
        or so it seemed;
Endlessly everything is different...
        or so it seems;
Tired night opens the heart.

SOLILOQUY IN ARREZO

Today, April 25th, we celebrate
The end of a more recent war
    in Latium;
(Not the one with Turnus and
    Pious Aeneas);
Also Sunday Mass with Piero
    della Francesca;
And then I step with parading
    Communists...

Tell them, please,
What he said:
Imposition of improvement
By decree
Usually engenders tyranny...
Though the playing band soothes;

Enough of war!
And tell them, please,
That—O too often—
An immoral war
Is one that lingers;
And we're not winning. . .
But the little boy drummer
Drums his drum. . .
And tell them, please,
What he said:
Homer and Polygnotus taught
That, properly speaking,
We are to reenact Hell
On earth. . .
And the old men sigh, though
No one sees. . .
Yet, tell them, please,
What Father Aeneas asked,
By the waters of Lethe:
O father! Is it possible
That any may be
So in love with life?. . .
I answer you, Aeneas,
Other than Anchises; and
Beg to report from
Chronicles II:
Because thine heart was tender.

THE WALLED TOWN THAT INSPIRED *THE INFERNO*

I
Within Monteriggioni, the turreted walls
For Dante's inspiration,
    Imagine,
       Please!—
Battalioned Florentines:
Gazing toward Siena;
Planning the most fecund of
    ecologies
(Plague-ridden carrion and feces).
 Chortling as their catapults
    roll south;
For they knew the truth:
The dark wind never
    blows north.

Dante terrifies...

II
Though if our fathers were but
        garbaging; we
Shall be the ecologists...
(Bombardier Beahan, and his crewmates,
        After Nagasaki,
            Tells the *Times*:
"We went to the club and had
  A few snorts...I
  Had really celebrated
  My birthday with a
  Big bang"; and
  Mr. Booz, and his workmates,
        Of du Pont,
            Tells the *Times*:
"Very little is known...
  Of chemical reactions
  In the upper
  Atmosphere"; and
  Dr. McElroy, and his thinkmates,
        Of Harvard,
            Tells the *Times*:
"It is a very unusual
  Situation for
  Science.")

Dante terrifies...

MOOD MUSIC FOR MIDSPRING

Though unprepared for the demise of May,
    When sudden summer is quickly sensed;
Though flowers yield their wanton bloom,
    Soon traveling bees are itinerant.

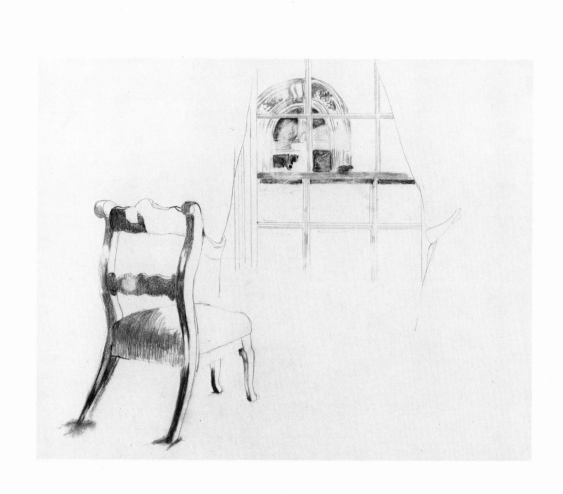

In the second barbarism, after the attempt at democracy, though they throng
together, they will live like wild beasts in a deep solitude of spirit;
and will, scarcely any two of them, be able to come to understanding. . .
like base savages under soft words and embraces.

Giambattista Vico

NOW THE UNKIND FLOURISH

In a Babel world of loving
Our self-love—I cannot hear you!
Fatigued inertia fortifies
The new religion; and benumbed
By an impercipient age,
We are led by those we lead.
Not even old doubting Dante
Is relevant; as the craven
Pursue the license of the self:
Only the unkind flourish
When mere thought leaves the floating words.

IN THE SECOND BARBARISM

Again the sun runs round our earth.

As gorged with import we demand
The scrubbings of our authority:
But emergings of the towered self
And stiflings of mediocrity.

We'd grasp the sureness of opinion
And expunge the doubting of the soul;
And then obviate the obvious—
That we are formed of formlessness.

HARKNESS

A soul on its nippled-heart must suck;
And only then may scan the harkness—
And affirm a reach of the febrile soul.
Know the nippled-heart to suck!

THE UNSEEN

But they who stand on
The left side of literature
Know so dutifully what to do:
Striving to be
The self-pitying one,
Mourning his lost Patroclus.
And like brilliant Achilles,
They wear a shield—
They've kissed a womb-God
Who defiled,
And taught her playing child
To be puerile.
Merely interring intellectuals,

Whose observations are
Always to be not trusted;
Whose hidden hearts are only
Acting lonely games—
Merely sure the heart's unseen.

VISITING A COMMUNE

Look look how strength is shown!
The time is always: aggression's here;
Only a lullaby said not to fear.
And memories of old desire,
Like constellations beyond our reach,
Caress experience's froward brow—
And fortify what we teach.

THE PREENING DOOR

O, let this damning world exalt
The Tigress of the Water Lilies;
And trembling dance before
The preening door: though
Her fantasies are on her face —
Derelict man delirious enter . . .

A LITIGIOUS SONNET

Your indictment says I cannot love!
And will sleep alone though many-bedded.
But I'd wait for a natural one,
And hope my love's a love whom I'd love.
A bill of particulars you'd present,
With many a grievance to cast around:
Then levy upon your angry suit
And marshal demands that I should care.
Are you not degree-ridden and journal-read?
Acquaintance-closeted and empty-dined?
With conventional grace and judging sighs,
In a court of love you'd have me fined.
Unshackled—without counsel—I'd appear;
My own brief presented: I'll wait till I care!

Staggering into middle age
And absenting myself
From assurèd ways,
I'd rest my head
On supportive care—
When will you be here?

I will not run with the most vulgar of all crowds, the literary. JOHN KEATS

UPON ASKING SOMEONE TO READ A POEM

"Not before lunch shall I read your poem!
The clock hasn't rung for delusion's time;
I didn't come to your languorous home
To brightly listen to your putrid rhyme!"

WHILE CONVERSING WITH A LITTLE GIRL

But how does one get to be so small?
By not being four, I'd guess.
For God and Goddess we pranced no less,
Not in vain remembered and still enthralled.

LUNCHING WITH MY LATIN TEACHER

And now you tell me you've grown old;
And even doors are difficult.
And now I tell you, "Those eyes are clear;
And that hasn't changed in twenty-three years."

Almost ninety. While we're having lunch,
Are you asking: "Is this a *tête-à-tête*"?
Carrying on in a feminine way:
"Shall I get fat from a pat of butter?"

And now you tell me all your news;
Twenty-three years was long ago.
And now I tell you all my news:
"I'm writing again . . . I'm writing again . . ."

And now you tell me, "It's so sad
 —No one knew that you were writing—"
And now I tell you, "I'm not mad";
And I lie to you in a gentle way.

You I wouldn't hurt (no tears at lunch).
It was only you who'd respond with feeling
And open my eyes to Ovid-caring;
While I poolroom-clowned and was hesitant.

And now you ask, "Would you read a poem?"
And say to me, "You were then a delight."
And now I remember drifting away . . .
While Virgil became adolescent play.

The progressive ones all knew what to say,
While I just sat there in a dreamy way;
And your teeth that were false went clickity-clack,
Like the lovely sounds of a streetcar track.

And now I read four of my poems,
And you brightly listen and quietly sit.
And now you say in a dreamy way:
"Poeta Nascitur non fit."

(Yes, tears at lunch.) "Oh, Lucile—once—
I walked long long in the wood!
Where blossoms stood on appled trees;
Fairy ships raced the dappled seas..."

THE TEMPEST

Ilona touched me!—but on the arm.
Her fingers barely grazed my cloth,
And now I know what Prosper knew:
Ilona touched me!—but for a while.

DUELING

"For Godsake, Ilona . . . enough!

"Then I challenge you to a duel—
  But now I will choose the weapons:
  Songbirds at twenty-seven feet."

"Poet," she shyly smiled at me—
"Then I shall choose another field:
  Dinner at home; seven-thirty."

Ilona's right . . . I haven't a chance—
And though, of course, we are but two:
I still would be but one with her.

THE REMAINDERMEN

Forgive the remaindermen, whose
Hireling hearts are beyond
The time of turning back;
Whose besieging hearts are appositioned
To the backward years;
And dream—O dream, now and then—
Of a time when love believed:
And no one asked why
The commitment to soft her.

While the moon is lit
In the mouth of the sky
Come—be my workmate!
With mortared passion
Build the considerate wall

One Rose, glassed in water
Airborne before me
Silently speaks among raucous limbs:
Philosopher to coincidence
Quietly, love

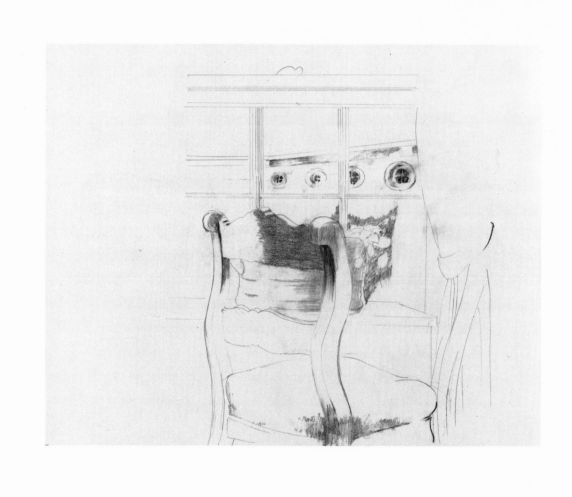

THE LOITERING WOLF MOON

And the loitering Wolf Moon winters slow
And the enveloping time gapes and laughs;
And the battled books scout relentlessly
And the picket sentinels lounge in row;
And I sit and think of no dearer time
And I know Ilona's melded here—
And all I dreamed were but dreams of her.

ILONA'S PAINTING!

Now freely go in circles
    —of one hundred degrees;
And rest your head on flowers
    —yet spleen the shoreless seas;
Gladiator of the heart!
Seek humbling beauty from the start.

THE ECONOMICS OF LOVE

. . . and now, dear love, elastic time
Heavies the air . . .
Waiting disintermediates
The coinage of our love.

Would you—a speculator—be
One half-hour late?
And, with time's inflation,
Risk the only gold money never raised?

And now, dear fulcrum of my happiness,
Shall I be condemned to feel;
But not to touch?
And now, dear love, I wait . . .

THE VISITING NURSE

I am six times the fool
And yet six times again the same!
To love one who gives to
Thirty-six others: Florence Flightingale,
Dressed in white,
Scours the city where men decay,
With hardly time for the thirty-seventh;
Who dreamt that he'd be other than
Supernumerary to a foster home—
As she lives a love as she has known.

THE WEDDING

Though dybbuks dance on a frosted cake
And bouquets of laughter line the aisle,
I precede myself with naivety—
Suited in arrogance of the unarmed.

And now: here comes the Gingerbread Lady!
And as I'm strewn about the garnished aisle,
Memories crowd the jewel box of my soul—
And I prepare to place grief's mantle on.

WHEN LOVE—MY LOVE—IS A PROXY CLAIM

Who may give his heart to leave it back
    And lonely walk the alluvian plain;
Who may bear delight in her glad act
    When love—my love—is a proxy claim.

The years should bring aptotic waters;
    No obscurants from another shore!
The years not spent in quiet quarters
    Brusk the age-with-beauty I adore.

INTERACTION OF THE FLOWERS

Petunias raise their lovely heads—
    I'd rather like to know:
Interaction of the flowers—
    While weeding, it's observed.

But I and you—we vine ourselves—
    Lashings to the ground;
And often brood the weight of us—
    Annuals we're not.

One Rose, bouqueted by others
Doomed by excess
And crowded from love

Now the dark wind shadows and I'm cold:
Her backward years rain inward tears
When a ghostly figure parapet-walks;
And I can hear what she cannot say
—What attracts is what repulses—
And her changeling heart has avenues
Revealing where I cannot walk.

And now I fear the termagant years...

NIGHT ON THE BEACH AT AMAGANSETT

Though endings down on me descend,
    The undertow bluffs the teasing sea;
Though wild wood flood to quickened tide,
    The tilted Dipper is vaguely spilt.

Unparented by the blurting world:
Things disorient the plunging sky,
And weary to bed I take my thoughts;
In tumbreled night I desperate lie.

EPIGRAPH FOR *OTHELLO*

Old woes new wail the keening sea—
On the raging crest of the primal tide

ON READING FREUD ON DaVINCI

What's in the artist's nature
That makes one course
The outward path?
And do not answer with jargon:
Telling of mere anger,
And unclaimed claims
And irretrievable
Wantings; nor tell
Of absent Odysseus
And tedious Telemachus'
Need to castrate
Her suitors; nor
Of waiting Laius!
Tell me why

Leonardo
Had the talent
Of Da Vinci—
Why can't you tell me
Even that?

                    still taunting,
        Emulous strides the stranger rock
                While
                        unreaching
        Repression grasps the strengthened twig
                    and hangs
                    Anxious

For that bird soaring in the sky
But undergoes a guarantee:
He shan't do more than you nor I;
Nor shape the lurch of destiny.

Let us plumb to the waiting sky!

TWO VARIATIONS ON A POEM / DREAM OF SIR HERBERT READ

I
THE LADY OF THE DREAM

Her Angel flight from cliff to lake
Sustains its poise upon the sheet of silk.

No ripples dim the surface as she falls
And, lake-received,
Her flesh redeems the rocky floor.

Quiet, she waits for one who dares
The level mirror of the lake.

II

THE DREAMER OF THE DREAM

Her Angel flight from cliff to lake
Sustains its poise upon the sheet of silk.

No ripples dim the surface as she falls
And, lake-received,
Her flesh redeems the rocky floor.

Quiet, she waits for those who dare
The level mirror of the lake.

O stranger in an anguished land!
Lain fallow on the rotting plain:
Quell the huge intruder
Who is wolf to man;
And climb the Island mountain
Wooded to a peak or two—
Cried-out beside the quarreling sky.

GROSSE FUGE IN B FLAT MAJOR

                    beyond allocable time,
Where madness screeches through steepled streets:
           The Virgin bless the sweeter boy
           And unchide the dissonant hours.

O give me time: beyond all thought!
Where strident sounds of the muted years
Are lost in cathedral embarrassment—
And no mad quartet is allocate.

MINGLING

I'll hawk my poems
On forbidden streets
In the silence of the day;
And lunge at readers in the soddy air
Then—mingling souls—
Sing the melody of childhood
Meadowland of time

A NOTE ON THE POET & ARTIST & TYPE

Daniel Haberman was born in New York City in 1933. Although he attended the Walden School, Carnegie-Mellon University and the graduate school of New York University, he was educated in the secondhand book shops of Manhattan; and by two years of study with Edward Dahlberg. He is associated with a typographic firm in Manhattan (where he lives) and is the designer of this book.

Cornelia Brendel Foss was born in Berlin, Germany. She received her early training in Italy, where she won first prize in the Rome International Sculpture Competition. She later studied in California and now paints in New York City and Long Island.

The type faces used are the calligraphic roman "Centaur" and the chancery cursive "Arrighi." They were revived by England's Bruce Rogers in 1914 and 1925 from original cuttings by Nicolaus Jensen and Ludovico degli Arrighi in 1470 and 1524 respectively. William Morris believed that "Jensen carried the development of roman type as far as it can go," and Rogers claimed that Arrighi italic is "one of the finest and most legible cursive letters ever produced." The composition was executed by a computer.